CORNISH
RECIPES
OLD AND NEW

ANN PASCOE

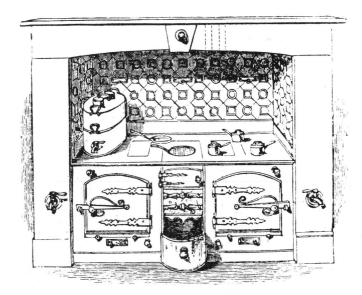

TOR MARK PRESS · PENRYN

Other books in this series

Publisher's note

The greatest care has been taken in the compilation of these recipes and all have been thoroughly tested. But as all experienced cooks will appreciate, cooking times may vary according, for example, to the depth of vessel or the efficiency of the oven.

Published by Tor Mark Press,
Islington Wharf, Penryn, Cornwall TR10 8AT

© 1988 Tor Mark Press

ISBN 0-85025-304-7

Printed in Great Britain by Cornwall Litho, Redruth

INTRODUCTION

Given an opportunity, the miners, farmworkers and fishermen of Cornwall during earlier centuries were prodigious eaters. The chance usually arose on days of national celebration when, by tradition, they were regaled by their employers with roast beef, plum pudding and strong beer. Such 'treats', however, were rare and normally their appetites had to be met by much plainer fare based principally on barley flour, the potato and the pilchard. In the poorest families it was ingenuity that introduced variety in the diet rather than a choice of ingredients, and this ingenuity is typical of traditional Cornish cookery as a whole.

The woman of the house usually had several means of cooking. The first of these was a huge iron crock used for soups and stews, kept suspended over the fire. There was also a baking iron, a metal sheet laid among the hot ashes and on which the food to be cooked was placed, and then covered with an iron 'baker'. There was also often a 'cloam' oven set in the wall of the huge chimney, dependent on the same fire for its heat.

Under the 'baker', or in the oven, were cooked the staple barley loaves—wheat flour was too dear—and the now widely acclaimed Cornish pasty. In olden days the latter was marked with the initial of its would-be consumer, since the contents of pasties varied, and still vary today, to suit all tastes—pork, rabbit, fish, eggs, vegetables and even jam or fruit. The initial end was always eaten last so that, should the pasty not be finished, it could be reclaimed by its owner. The proper pasty, however, filled with potatoes, turnip and a little meat, was a meal in itself. For this reason it was most convenient to take into the fields or down the mine for consumption at 'croust' time. Also made of barley flour, the traditional pasty of former centuries was heavy and hard—hard enough, so it is said, to be dropped down a mine shaft without breaking!

The labouring poor could afford little to flavour and diversify their starchy and heavy diet of potatoes and bread. The principal exception was the Cornish pilchard. This was caught and salted down by the tens of thousands in the autumn, although sometimes the harvest failed, whilst in particularly hard times even the fish salt, made locally or brought from France, was too costly. The pilchard was prepared and served a dozen or more different ways, many of which would be considered unpalatable today. Yet there were other fish to be caught by those who lived along the coast: gurnet and conger, mackerel, herring, even crab and lobster perhaps, while in hungry times even limpets found their way into the cooking pot. Legitimately or otherwise, on occasion the odd woodpigeon, rabbit, curlew or cormorant, trout, duck, rook, thrush or pheasant lay quietly simmering beneath a tasty pie crust. Goose, too, was not uncommon, since these were widely reared on the moors and rough ground where tin streaming took place.

Other recurring features in the diet of earlier days were cream, and meat from the ubiquitous Cornish pig. The former was naturally a luxury, the latter less so, since most families contrived to keep at least one pig. Use was made, although no doubt very sparingly, of almost every part of the animal, resulting in such Cornish specialities as grovey cake, hog's pudding and the dubious pleasures of muggety pie. Where necessary—and when the required salt could be afforded—portions of the carcase were preserved immediately after slaughter, for use during the coming year in the form of ham, bacon or pork.

It is unlikely that many visitors leave Cornwall today without having tasted its most delectable cream, yet in former days the enjoyment of this delicacy was reserved only for those of comfortable means. Poorer families had to content themselves with skimmed milk or occasionally even thin cream or 'dippy' but, given the chance, like their betters they too would enjoy dollops of clotted cream, not only with splits and sandwiches, fried eggs and brandy snaps, pies and pasties, but even with pilchards and potatoes.

SOUPS

FISH SOUP

1 small haddock or whiting	$\frac{3}{4}$ pint milk
1 onion, medium size	2 ozs butter
Pepper and salt	

Put the fish into a saucepan with the onion (finely chopped), seasoning and $1\frac{1}{2}$ pints of water. Simmer for about half an hour until the fish breaks up easily. Drain off and save the fish stock. Shred the fish finely, removing any skin or bones, and place in a pan with the butter, milk and fish stock. Reheat and simmer for ten minutes. If a slightly thicker soup is preferred $1\frac{1}{2}$ ozs of flour mixed with a little milk can be added. Add a little finely chopped parsley before serving.

POTATO SOUP

2 lbs potatoes	1 quart milk
1 large onion	$\frac{1}{2}$ oz flour
1 oz bacon fat	1 cup milk
Seasoning	

Melt the bacon fat in a saucepan and cook the chopped onion in this without browning until tender (about 5 or 10 minutes). Add the stock, the peeled and finely diced potatoes and the seasoning. Bring to the boil and simmer gently for about 20 to 30 minutes. Blend the flour to a smooth cream with the milk, stir in and bring the soup back to the boil for 2 or 3 minutes. Serve piping hot.

KETTLE OR KIDDLY BROTH

3 onions
1¾ ozs dripping
Pepper and salt

1 quart of water or stock
Stale bread
1 rasher bacon (or several bacon rinds)

Peel and cut up the onions and simmer in the water with the bacon and dripping for about an hour. Sieve the soup and pour on to the stale bread, cut into cubes. Season well and eat very hot.

LEEK AND POTATO SOUP

1 lb potatoes
2 large leeks
1 rasher bacon
Salt and pepper

$\frac{3}{4}$ pint stock
$\frac{1}{4}$ pint milk
$\frac{1}{2}$ oz butter

Chop the bacon up small and fry lightly in a saucepan. Add the butter, sliced leeks and potatoes. Cook on a gentle heat until the vegetables are tender. Add the stock, season well and cover. Simmer for a further 20 minutes. Finally add the milk to the soup just before serving, re-heat and re-season if necessary.

NETTLE SOUP

2 lbs young nettles
1¼ lbs spinach
1½ pints good stock
Cold milk

4 cold cooked sausages
3 tbsps sour cream
3 tbsps flour
Seasoning

Gather the tips of young stinging nettles, wearing gloves. Wash and blanch the nettles. Wash the spinach. Boil the stock and pour this over the nettles and the spinach. Season and simmer for about three quarters of an hour, adding further stock if required. Pass the liquid through a sieve, then add the flour blended to a cream with a little cold milk. Boil up to thicken, add the sausages chopped up into small rounds and, just before serving, the sour cream.

WATERCRESS AND POTATO SOUP

About $\frac{1}{2}$ lb potatoes	$\frac{1}{2}$ pint warmed milk
2 bunches watercress	1 oz butter
Salt and pepper	1 oz flour
3 tbsps cold milk	2 thin slices white bread

Boil the potatoes and drain them, saving the potato water. Sieve the potatoes into a pan and add $\frac{3}{4}$ pint of the potato water. Chop the watercress, warm $\frac{1}{2}$ pint of milk and add to the potatoes. Season. Make a smooth paste with the flour and the cold milk and add to the soup. Boil for a few minutes, then float the butter on top. Toast some thinly sliced bread, remove the crusts, cut into small squares and either sprinkle on the soup or serve dry, separately.

FISH DISHES

HERRING PIE

6 herrings
1½ lbs potatoes
½ pint milk
Pickled nasturtium seeds
or gherkins

3 large tomatoes
2 cupfuls fine white
breadcrumbs
Pepper

The herrings should be those pickled in brine. Clean and bone the fish and soak overnight. In the morning skin the herrings, cook over boiling water until tender, drain, and flake the flesh, Add a couple of chopped gherkins or a few pickled nasturtium seeds, pepper, (no salt), and milk. Do not make the mixture too wet. Put the tomatoes in boiling water for a few minutes, skin them, allow to cool and slice. Place the fish in an ovenproof dish, arrange the slices of tomatoes on top, then the mashed potato. Bake for 40 minutes at 375°F.

Herrings always provide a cheap, nutritious meal which is very flavoursome. They are best eaten from June to December.

BAKED GURNET

4 gurnet, washed and cleaned
A medium sized onion
Pepper and salt
A little white wine if desired

1 tomato
A small lemon
½ oz butter

Cut the fins and the head off the fish, score the skin, season well and place in a fireproof dish. Soak the tomato in very hot water for a minute or two, then peel. Cut the onion, the centre portion of the lemon and the peeled tomato into thin slices and arrange over the fish. Season again and top with a few knobs of butter. Add a cupful of white wine if desired, and bake for about half an hour at 400°F.

There are two types of gurnet, red and grey, of which the first is the best. The fish is a bright lobster red, with a very large head, but the flesh is white, flavoursome and firm. It is at its best from July to April.

MARINATED PILCHARDS

Allow two or three pilchards per person. Clean the fish, washing each one very thoroughly inside and put in a bay leaf with plenty of pepper and salt. Place in an enamel or earthenware glazed dish and pour on enough vinegar to cover the fish. Put on a lid, or tie on a sheet of greaseproof paper, and bake at about 300°F until the bones of the fish are completely soft. Serve cold. Mackerel and herring can be prepared in the same way.

DIPPY

6 pilchards   Thin cream
$1\frac{1}{2}$ lbs potatoes

Clean the fish, peel and cut up the potatoes and simmer both in thin cream in a pan until soft.

NIFLIN AND POTATOES

Boiled niflin (Newfoundland cod fish) was frequently eaten in the old days with potatoes baked in their skins. The dish was much improved by a few spoonfuls of dippy (thin cream) run over the potatoes.

HERRING ROES

Wash the roes thoroughly, dry them and roll in seasoned flour. Melt some butter, run this over the roes and grill. Sprinkle with lemon juice and serve on toast.

BAKED RED MULLET

6 red mullet	Lemon juice
About 2 ozs butter	Pepper and salt
Few sprigs parsley	

Clean the fish, leaving in the liver, which is very choice, and remove the eyes and fins. Arrange in a greased baking dish, season and sprinkle with lemon juice. Bake at 400°F for about 30 minutes, either under greaseproof paper or with a lid. As the flesh is very likely to break when lifted many people prefer to wrap each fish individually in greased paper. This makes them easier to remove on to a serving plate. Arrange on a flat dish and garnish with thin lemon slices and parsley. Put a sprig of parsley in each eye socket. Serve with a good rich parsley sauce.

As with gurnet there are both red and grey types, of which the red is the best. It was once caught in great quantities off the Land's End coasts.

BAKED WHITING

6 small whiting	Golden breadcrumbs
1 oz melted butter	Lemon slices
Parsley sprigs	

Clean and skin the fish, cutting out the eyes with a pair of sharp scissors (the modern way is then to make a circle of each fish, passing the tail through both eye sockets). Brush with butter, season, and sprinkle with crumbs. Bread leftovers, dried in the oven and rolled can be used instead. Arrange in a greased dish, place a knob of butter on each fish, and bake for 30 minutes at 350°F. Place on a round serving dish and garnish with lemon and parsley.

Whiting poached in milk is very good for a delicate stomach, as it is easily digested. This fish is best eaten between December and March.

LIMPETS

Wash and scrub very thoroughly in running water and then boil until the flesh comes out of the shell. Drain, cool and serve with plenty of pepper and vinegar.

BAKED SEA BREAM

Clean the fish, scrape off the coarse scales and prepare a stuffing with equal quantities of shredded suet and seasoned fine breadcrumbs. Chop some parsley and add to the stuffing. Place this inside the fish, put on a greased baking tray, dot with butter and bake for 30 minutes at 350°F.

Bream is in season from June to December and has a very delicate flavour.

POACHED BREAM IN SAUCE

Bream is also excellent poached in water and served with a white sauce. Make the sauce by simmering a slice of onion, half an inch thick and finely chopped, in a little milk. Melt a knob of butter in a pan, add a little flour (about half an ounce of each) and then add the milk and onion, cooking until it thickens. Beat in two dessertspoonfuls of a good mayonnaise, preferably home-made, and pour over the fish in a serving dish.

WHITEBAIT

These little fish (small fry of shoaling fish such as herring or mackerel) need no cleaning other than a good wash. Allow half a pound of fish per person. Dry thoroughly and roll in seasoned flour or breadcrumbs. Plunge into very hot, deep fat a few at a time. They will then be very brown and crisp, which is important, and are best served with a good squeeze of lemon juice.

FISH CAKES

8 ozs haddock, boiled	Salt and pepper
8 ozs mashed potatoes	1 beaten egg
Parsley	Flour
Golden crumbs	

Mix the mashed potatoes with the cooked fish after it has been skinned, boned and flaked. Add a little chopped parsley plus the salt and pepper. Roll into small, flat cakes on a floured board. Brush with egg, roll in the crumbs and fry for about 10 minutes, turning once.

MACKEREL WITH GOOSEBERRIES

6 mackerel	$\frac{3}{4}$ lb gooseberries
4 ozs butter	Seasoned flour
Nutmeg	Parsley

Melt 3 ozs of the butter in a large frying pan, roll the fish in seasoned flour and cook in the butter till tender. Or they can be roasted in the oven. Stew the gooseberries in a little water and sugar. Melt 1 oz of butter in a pan, add the gooseberries with a dash of nutmeg and some chopped parsley. Season to taste and serve with the mackerel.

SOUSED HERRINGS

6 herrings
3 bay leaves
Vinegar
9 peppercorns

1 medium sized onion
Salt and black pepper
Parsley

Clean, scale and bone the fish. Lay flat on a board. Place on each one or two thin slices of onion, season and roll up, starting at the head end. Place in an ovenproof dish, packing tightly to prevent unrolling. Place half a bay leaf between each two fish, cover with vinegar and water (one part of each) and add the peppercorns and chopped parsley. Bake at 350°F for about an hour and allow to cool. They are very good served with the liquid but a longer baking will reduce this and make the fish drier and crisper for those who prefer it.

CHEESE AND FISH PIE

1 lb boiled cod
½ pint fish stock
1 oz onion, finely chopped
1 oz parsley, chopped
Salt and pepper
1 tsp mustard
½ tsp cayenne pepper

1 oz flour
1 oz butter
2 ozs grated cheese
2 lbs potatoes
Worcester sauce
Vinegar

Cover the fish with cold water, bring to the boil and simmer until tender. Drain, saving the liquid. Remove the skin and bones from the fish while still warm, and flake the flesh. Fry the onion in the butter on a low heat until soft. Add the flour, stirring, and then the stock (milk can be used as part of the quantity). Bring to the boil, simmer until it thickens, stirring all the while. Add the salt and pepper, the dry mustard, and a few drops each of Worcester sauce and vinegar, and the parsley and cheese. Mix in the flaked fish, turn in to a greased ovenproof dish and top with the potatoes nicely mashed and creamed. Put the dish in a moderate oven for about 15 minutes and serve piping hot.

MUSSELS IN CREAM SAUCE

1 pint fresh mussels	2 tbsps thin fresh cream
$\frac{1}{2}$ pint prepared stock	Salt and pepper
(see below)	Yolk of an egg
Parsley	

Scrub the mussels under water most thoroughly (the shells should be closed when bought). Prepare the stock by taking half a pint of water, and adding a little salt and pepper, 1 tsp of vinegar, a pinch of mixed herbs, 1 clove and a piece each of, carrot, celery and onion. Simmer until the vegetables are soft, allow to cool, and strain. Then place the mussels in the stock and bring to the boil, gently agitating the pan. When the shells open remove the mussels, cut away the beard and lay each on a dish, each resting in half the shell. Cover with a cloth or lid. Simmer the stock for five minutes, allow to cool a little and gradually add the beaten eggs and cream. Re-heat gently and pour over the shellfish. Garnish with parsley.

STEWED SCALLOPS IN MILK

Take the scallops out of their shells and wash and dry carefully. Discard the black portion and the beard. Put a little milk in a pan and simmer the flesh in this for about 10 minutes. Make a white sauce, using the milk; pour this over the scallops in a serving dish and garnish with parsley and lemon slices.

These shellfish are best eaten between October and March, and preferably in January and February. They have a white flesh and an orange roe and must be very fresh.

BAKED SCALLOPS

Scallops are just as tasty baked in the oven. Take them out of the shells, throw half of these away and well scrub the rest. Wash the scallops, removing the dark part and the beard. Cut the edible flesh into small pieces, placing this in the remaining shells. Sprinkle lemon juice and golden crumbs over the scallops, add small pieces of butter then bake for 30 minutes at 350°F. A sheet of greaseproof paper placed over them in the oven will prevent drying out.

CRAB

A live crab must be plunged in deep boiling water, well salted, to kill it. Boil for about twenty minutes, drain and cool. Over-cooking will harden the flesh. Remember that the claw meat is white and that in the shell brown, so if choosing a ready cooked crab bear your family's preference in mind. Most people would select a male crab, which has large claws and a small body. Shake the crab before buying and reject it if it sounds to contain water.

To dress, place the crab on its back and pull off the claws. Separate the top shell from the body of the crab. Take the shell, discard the stomach bag (just below the head) and scrape out and save all the brown meat. Take the body, discard the grey 'dead man's fingers', remove and save the white flesh. Crack the larger claws and remove all the white meat. Season the brown flesh with vinegar, salt and pepper, and chopped parsley. Mix with a few white breadcrumbs. Take the shell, break away the underside as far as the dark line near the edge and fill the outside with brown meat. Mix together all the white meat, season as above and fill the centre of the shell with this. Garnish with parsley.

MEAT DISHES

CORNISH UNDER ROAST

1 lb good quality steak
Raw potatoes cut into
large pieces

1 large sliced onion
Seasoning

Cut the meat into strips, removing any excess fat. Dip each one in seasoned flour and roll up. Arrange rolls on the bottom of a dish and cover with sliced onions. Add the potatoes, one or two pieces of fat cut off the meat and almost cover the contents of the dish with cold water. Cook in a moderate oven for at least one hour.

TOAD IN THE HOLE

1 egg
$\frac{1}{2}$ pint of milk
5 or 6 sausages

4 ozs flour
Pinch of salt

Mix the flour and the salt together thoroughly. Make a well in the centre and break an egg into this. Gradually add $\frac{1}{4}$ pint of the milk, mixing meanwhile to a smooth batter. Beat the batter for about five minutes until full of air bubbles and then incorporate the remaining milk. Put one tablespoonful of beef dripping in a shallow tin, together with five or six sausages. Place in a hot oven and when the fat is smoking pour on the creamy batter. Cook at 450°F for about 40 minutes.

TOAD IN THE HOLE (ECONOMICAL)

1 lb well flavoured sausage
    meat
1½ lbs potatoes
½ oz margarine or butter

Seasoning
Some made mustard
Potato water

Roll the sausage meat into tiny balls and flatten each one. Boil the potatoes, strain and save the potato water. Add the seasoning and butter to the potatoes, mash thoroughly, then whip with a fork. Add a little of the potato water or, preferably, milk. Make a thick layer with this potato in the bottom of a greased dish, spread the mustard on one side of each round of sausage, then lay it mustard side down on the potato. Cook at 350°F for about half an hour, until the whole is golden brown.

HOG'S PUDDING

Some of the best recipes for this traditional Cornish dish have been handed down over the generations by Cornish pork butchers, and are well guarded secrets. Here is one of them.

Soak some pig skins in salted water. Mix together minced pork, bread crumbs and a sprinkling of mixed herbs. Season thoroughly with salt and pepper. Fill the skins with this mixture and tie the ends of each tightly. Boil until cooked.

Hog's pudding is delicious sliced and eaten cold, fried with bacon, bread or egg, or even put into a Cornish pasty.

BACON AND PARSLEY PIE

Bunch of parsley
Shortcrust pastry
Pepper and salt

3 hard-boiled eggs
6 rashers of bacon

Line a deep pie-dish with the pastry. Boil the parsley, drain and place half the amount in the dish. Add the bacon, cut up into pieces, the hard-boiled eggs, peeled and flaked, plenty of seasoning and rest of the parsley. Cover with good meat stock, add a lid of pastry and bake at 450°F until nicely browned.

RAW FRY

6 slices streaky bacon	3 large potatoes
1 large onion	Salt and pepper

Fry the bacon, using a deep frying pan, and adding the onion before the bacon is completely cooked. Fry gently for a further 3 to 5 minutes. Then add the thinly sliced potatoes, salt and pepper, and cold water to within about half an inch of the top. Cover with a lid and simmer until the potatoes are soft.

Potato jowdle is another version of this but omits the bacon.

WHOLE MEAT MOULD

1 lb stewing beef	1 carrot
1 onion	Salt
1 small turnip	Black pepper
1 stalk celery	Bouquet garni

Remove any excess fat off the meat and place the latter in a pan of water without cutting it up at all. Peel and cut up the vegetables and put these, with the bouquet garni, either into a pressure cooker basket or in a muslin bag. Place this in the pan with the meat and cover tightly. Simmer on a very low heat for about three hours, topping up the water if need be. Allow to cool slightly, remove the vegetables and herbs, and transfer the meat into a mould, packing down tightly. Add sufficient of the liquor just to cover and then place on the top of the meat a saucer or plate of the right size. Weight this down and put the dish into a cool place until morning. It can then be up-ended and the meat mould turned out.

PIG'S TROTTERS

4 pig's trotters

2 lbs potatoes

1 medium turnip

2 large carrots

2 large onions

4 pints water

Seasoning

Thyme and parsley

Clean the trotters and blanch by putting them in boiling water for a few minutes. Peel and slice the carrots, onions and turnip. Place them in a pan with the water and add the trotters, parsley and thyme. Bring to the boil and simmer for about two hours. Remove the trotters and cut off all the meat. Place this in the pan again, together with the potatoes, thinly sliced. Bring once more to the boil and simmer for a further 40 minutes.

MEAT FUGGAN

1 lb flour

4 ozs lard

Salt

About 6 ozs meat, finely cubed and seasoned

Sieve the flour and the salt together and rub in the lard. Mix with water to a dry dough and form into the shape of a large fat pasty. Make a slit down the centre, open it wide and put in the meat. Close the cut, nipping the sides together, and bake for 40 minutes at 450°F.

BACON AND POTATO PIE

8 rashers bacon

$\frac{1}{2}$ lb potatoes

1 oz onion

$\frac{1}{2}$ cupful milk

1 oz flour

2 eggs

$\frac{1}{2}$ oz dripping

Seasoning

Cut off the bacon rinds and chop the bacon into small pieces. Peel the potatoes and shred very fine. Drain thoroughly. Finely chop the onion. Mix all three together and add the flour. Beat the eggs, add the salt, pepper and milk, and blend this liquid into the bacon, onion and potato mixture. Melt the dripping in a shallow tin until smoking hot, pour in the mixture and bake at 400°F for about three quarters of an hour. Cut up like Yorkshire pudding and serve hot, in slices, topped with a dollop of Cornish cream and accompanied by fresh green peas.

ROAST MEAT AND POTATO CREAM CAKE

1 lb potatoes	Black pepper
2 medium onions	Salt
1 gill double cream	Ground nutmeg
Shortcrust pastry	

Peel the potatoes and onions and slice very thinly. Season well. Place in a colander, cover, and allow to drain for about half an hour. Put a pie-funnel in the centre of a round greased baking tin. Arrange the onion and potato slices in the tin, cover with a shortcrust pastry lid and bake for about half an hour at 425°F. Pour the cream through the funnel and serve the dish with roast meat (beef or lamb, preferably), or on its own for supper.

MEAT PASTY

1 lb shortcrust pastry	6 ozs potatoes
12 ozs raw mutton or steak	1 small onion, chopped
3 tbsps cold water	Seasoning

Make the pastry and roll out to about a quarter of an inch thick. Cut into rounds, using a saucer or a small plate. Cut up the meat into small pieces, rejecting anything inedible such as gristle, lumps of fat, or bone. Dice the raw potato and finely chop the onion. Mix the meat, onion and potato together very thoroughly, add salt and pepper and about three tablespoonfuls of cold water. Place some of this filling on one half of each circle of pastry, damp the edges of the latter with cold water and fold over to cover the mixture. Press the edges of the pastry together and crimp it with the fingers to seal. Make two or three ventilating slits in the 'lid', brush with beaten egg or milk if a glaze is required, and place on a baking tray. Cook in a hot oven (450°F) until the pastry is pale brown, then reduce the heat to 350-375°F for about 40 minutes.

HERB PASTY

Chop and scald a quantity of well washed parsley, watercress and spinach. Cut up finely some shallots or leeks and one or two rashers of bacon. Place the vegetables and bacon on rounds of pastry (see above), crimp each pasty except at one point and pour into this a small amount of beaten egg. Seal the pasties and bake as usual.

BACON AND EGG PASTY

Take three slices of streaky bacon and one hard-boiled egg to each pasty. Rind and dice the bacon, add the egg, shelled and flaked, as well as the chopped parsley, pepper and salt.

Bacon and turnip pasty is equally good, especially if eaten with Cornish cream.

LEEK (LICKY) PASTY

Remove the dark green heads of the leeks, slice the remainder and wash thoroughly in cold water to remove any grit. The leeks will make a satisfactory filling with a few small knobs of butter and a good sprinkling of pepper and salt. A little chopped bacon can also be added.

HOG'S PUDDING PASTY

Make as for meat pasty but substitute some skinned and diced hog's pudding for the steak or mutton.

APPLE AND FIGGY PASTY

Diced raw apple with brown sugar and a few figs ('Cornish' for raisins) make a good filling. Sprinkle with water to moisten before closing the pasty. A little powdered cinnamon may be added instead of the raisins.

FISH PASTY

Simmer some fish, say herring or mackerel, until the flesh is soft enough to part from the bones. Leave to cool, then remove the skin and bones, and flake the fish. Divide this up on to pastry rounds, adding finely chopped parsley, and seasoning. Bake in a hot oven.

TURNIP PASTY

Pasties can be made using finely diced turnip as the filling, with plenty of pepper and a good lump of butter. Serve hot. Diced turnip can also be put into meat pasty, reducing the amount of potato accordingly. For a tasty economical pasty, the filling can be entirely of diced potato, with plenty of seasoning and a spoonful of butter or fresh cream.

PIES

CONGER PIE

Conger eels are best eaten in autumn and winter, and small ones are preferable. Cut off the head, skin and wash the eel and slice into small steaks, if possible using only the centre of the fish. Coat the pieces in seasoned flour and place in a greased dish with chopped parsley, seasoning and knobs of butter. Half fill the dish with milk and cook in a medium oven until the fish is partly done. Then add a shortcrust pastry lid and place in a hot oven to complete the cooking. This dish is nice when eaten with fresh cream.

SQUAB PIE

Cut half a pound of mutton or veal into small cubes. Line the bottom of a pie dish with these and cover with a layer of sliced apples. Sprinkle with sugar, then add a few slices of onion. Season, then add a layer of currants or sultanas and a little mixed spice. Continue in this way until the dish is three-quarters full, finishing with a covering of sliced apples. Add some meat stock and cover with a pastry lid. Bake until the meat is tender.

RABBIT AND KNUCKLE PIE

Joint the rabbit and knuckle, and simmer in a pan with seasoning for about an hour. Then add thinly sliced raw potato and chopped parsley, cooking these until tender. Transfer all to a deep ovenproof dish, provide a shortcrust pastry lid and cook at 450°F until this is well browned.

MUGGETY PIE

Thoroughly clean the intestines of a pig, cut up and lay them in a greased dish with a covering of sliced onions. Season well. Add a pastry lid and bake about one hour.

LEEKY PIE

6 leeks
4 rashers bacon
4 eggs
1 oz butter

Salt and pepper
Marjoram
Shortcrust pastry

Trim the heads of the leeks, cut into short lengths and wash very thoroughly in plenty of water to remove any grit. Cut the bacon rashers into small pieces, place these with a little water and the leeks in a pan and cook gently until the leeks are almost tender. Transfer into an ovenproof dish, add the salt, pepper, butter and a little marjoram. Break the eggs into a bowl and beat them, then pour them over the leeks and bacon in the dish. Cover with a shortcrust pastry lid and bake at 475°F until the pastry is nicely brown.

PIGEON PIE

3 pigeons
12 ozs steak (or 6 ozs each
    of veal and ham)
4 ozs breadcrumbs
3 hard-boiled eggs

Nutmeg
Lemon rind
Plenty of salt and
    pepper
Cayenne pepper
Jelly stock

Bone the pigeons and cut up the flesh. Trim and mince the meat, add the breadcrumbs, all the seasonings and lemon rind, and mix together. Line a dish with this mixture, and fill the centre with pigeon meat and the chopped eggs. Add the jelly stock, cover with a layer of the meat and breadcrumb mixture and add a pastry lid. Bake at about 475°F until the pastry is brown, cover with greaseproof paper to prevent the pastry from burning, and then cook a further 2 hours at a lower temperature until the meat is tender.

STAR-GAZY PIE

6 pilchards	Seasoning
2 or 3 hard-boiled eggs	Shortcrust pastry

Take half a dozen pilchards, mackerel or herrings. Remove any scales, and clean and bone the fish. The heads must be left on. Season the inside of each fish, place them all in a greased dish with the flaked hard-boiled eggs and cover the whole with a pastry lid. Make slits in the pastry and arrange the heads of the fish to 'star-gaze' through these. Alternatively, the heads can be removed at the beginning and placed in the slits in the pastry separately.

HERBY PIE

Chop and scald some watercress, shallots or leaks, parsley and spinach. Put a layer of bacon on the bottom and round the sides of a greased dish. Fill with the herbs mixed with two well beaten eggs, then top off with several more rashers of bacon. Provide the whole with a thin lid of shortcrust pastry and bake in a moderate oven (350°F) for at least an hour.

CREAMS & CREAM DISHES

CORNISH CLOTTED CREAM

Choose a wide, shallow earthenware pan. Strain very fresh milk into this and leave to stand, overnight if summertime or for twenty-four hours in cold weather. Then slowly, and without simmering, raise the temperature of the milk over a low heat until a solid ring starts to form around the edge. Without shaking the pan, very carefully remove it from the heat and leave overnight, or a little longer, in a cool place. The thick crust of cream can then be skimmed off the surface with a large spoon or a fish-slice.

CURDS AND CREAM

Take one pint of cold milk and add a little lemon juice. Heat very carefully and slowly, without boiling, until a curd forms. Filter through a muslin cloth to allow the liquid whey to drain through, and then serve the curds cold with Cornish cream and a sprinkling of castor sugar.

SYLLABUB

1 pint double cream
4 tbsps sherry
4 tbsps brandy

2 lemons
6 ozs castor sugar

Grate and juice the lemons and leave the peel to stand in the juice for several hours. Whip the cream thoroughly. Add the brandy and sherry to the lemon juice, and then the sugar, stirring until dissolved. Carefully blend this liquid with the cream, adding a little at a time until a soft, smooth curd is produced. Serve very cold and not too much per person, as it is very rich. Syllabub at one time was made with cider or ale, and creamy milk, well spiced, and was then less filling.

CREAMED APPLE

Bake half a dozen nice apples, scoop out the insides and pass them through a sieve. Add a generous half cupful of cream and one tablespoonful of lemon juice. Beat in three tablespoonfuls of sieved castor sugar and serve chilled.

CAKES & BISCUITS

FIGGY 'OBBIN (FIGGY DUFF)

8 ozs suet
1 lb flour
1 tsp salt

2 tsps baking powder
Cold water

Mix together the suet, flour, salt and baking powder. Add water gradually to form a dry, elastic dough. Knead lightly and roll out to half an inch thick. Sprinkle on two handfuls of figs ('Cornish' for raisins), roll them in lightly and then fold up, like a jam suet pudding, sealing the ends. Criss-cross the top with a knife, brush with milk and dust with sugar. Bake at 350°F for about half an hour. Best eaten hot.

GROVEY CAKE

Grovey cake was made at pig-killing time, the groves being the dry, brown pieces of pork fat after it was rendered down for lard. They were mixed with barley flour and salt, baked, cut into squares and eaten hot.

POTATO CAKE

1 lb potatoes
Salt and pepper

1 oz butter
3 ozs flour

Boil the potatoes and mash them with the seasoning and the butter. Gradually mix in the flour. Roll out on a floured board to about half an inch thick. Cut into small shapes if required and cook on a hot, greased girdle or in a frying pan for about 15 minutes, turning once. Serve very hot with plenty of butter. Cold leftover mashed potatoes can be used but the cake will be heavier and less digestible.

HEAVY CAKE

1 lb flour	12 ozs currants
4 ozs butter	6 ozs sugar
4 ozs lard	$\frac{1}{2}$ tsp salt
About $\frac{1}{4}$ pint milk	

Rub the lard in the flour and add the salt, sugar and fruit. Mix to a soft dough with the milk. Turn on to a floured board and roll out to a long strip about 6 inches wide. Distribute half the butter in small pieces over the top two-thirds of the pastry. Fold the bottom third without fat upwards and then the top third down over it. Give the pastry a half turn so that the folds are at the sides. Roll out again into a thin strip and spread the rest of the butter as before, repeating the folding in the same way. Roll out finally into a square about half an inch thick. Score the top into a lattice pattern, brush with egg and bake for about thirty minutes at 400°F.

LAUNCESTON CAKE

6 ozs butter	1 lb currants
6 ozs sugar	2 ozs lemon peel
8 ozs flour	$\frac{1}{2}$ tbsp black treacle
2 ozs ground almonds	1 tbsp golden syrup
3 eggs	

Cream the sugar and fat, add the treacle, syrup and then the eggs one at a time, beating each one in thoroughly before adding the next. Lastly, mix together the flour, almonds, currants and lemon peel, and fold them carefully into the mixture. Bake at 350°F for about 90 minutes.

CORNISH GINGERBREADS

4 ozs demerara sugar
4 ozs butter
12 ozs white flour

8 ozs black treacle or syrup
$\frac{3}{4}$ oz ground ginger
$\frac{1}{2}$ oz bicarbonate of soda

Mix together the sugar, butter and treacle until creamy and light. Sieve the flour and ginger together and add, mixing in lightly. Warm a little milk, dissolve in it the bicarbonate of soda, and mix thoroughly with the rest. Turn the mixture on to a floured board, divide into small pieces and roll into balls between floured hands. Place several inches apart on a greased baking tray. Cook for about ten minutes in a hot oven.

GINGERBREAD

1 lb white flour
8 ozs brown sugar
6 ozs butter
12 ozs treacle
1 egg
$\frac{1}{2}$ tsp bicarbonate of soda

$\frac{1}{2}$ tsp salt
$1\frac{1}{2}$ tsps ground ginger
$\frac{1}{2}$ oz lemon peel
$\frac{1}{2}$ pint milk
2 tsps baking powder

Sieve the flour, salt, baking powder, bicarbonate of soda and ginger together. Add the finely grated lemon peel. Put the butter, treacle and sugar into a pan and melt gently over a low heat. Beat the egg and add this to the warmed milk. Mix all the ingredients together very thoroughly and divide into tiny balls rolled round in the palms. Space widely on a greased baking tray and cook for about 10 minutes at 400°F.

PORTER CAKES

8 ozs butter	1 lb flour
12 ozs sugar	$1\frac{1}{2}$ lbs currants
2 eggs	$\frac{1}{2}$ tsp mixed spice
$\frac{1}{2}$ pint stout	1 tsp bicarbonate of soda

Melt the butter over very gentle heat and when turned to oil add the sugar, stout and well beaten eggs. Mix the fruit in the flour and add this. Lastly add the bicarbonate of soda and the mixed spice and stir thoroughly for several minutes. Divide into equal parts and bake in two tins at about 350°F for at least two hours.

FARMHOUSE CAKE

8 ozs white flour	1 oz chopped candied
8 ozs wholemeal flour	peel
8 ozs sugar	$\frac{1}{2}$ tsp mixed spice
4 ozs raisins	$\frac{1}{2}$ tsp bicarbonate of soda
4 ozs sultanas	1 egg
6 ozs butter	Milk

Sieve together the white and brown flours, the spice and the bicarbonate of soda. Rub in the fat. Add the peel, fruit and sugar. Mix in the egg and milk to a dropping consistency and bake for about two hours at 400°F to 425°F.

FUGGAN

1 lb flour	4 ozs raisins or currants
Good pinch of salt	4 ozs lard
Water	

Sift the flour and the salt together, rub in the fat and add the fruit. Add water to form a soft dough, not too sticky, shape into a thick oval and mark in a lattice pattern with a knife. Bake for 25 to 30 minutes.

APPLE DICKY

1 lb flour
4 ozs lard
Water

2 or 3 apples
Good pinch of salt

Sift the flour and the salt together, rub in the fat and add the apples, peeled and cut up. Add sufficient water to make a dry, elastic dough and roll out flat. Bake for about half an hour.

SEEDY CAKE

4 ozs sugar
4 ozs butter
2 eggs
Milk

6 ozs flour
$\frac{1}{2}$ tsp baking powder
Salt
1 tsp caraway seeds

Cream the butter and sugar together, then add and beat in the eggs one at a time. Sieve together the flour, baking powder and the salt, and add the caraway seeds. Fold into the creamed butter, sugar and eggs, adding enough milk to make the mixture drop off a spoon. Bake for about 60 minutes at 400°F.

CORNISH TEA CAKES

8 ozs self raising flour
4 ozs beef dripping
4 ozs currants
$\frac{1}{2}$ tsp mixed spice

1 oz candied peel
2 ozs sugar
$\frac{1}{2}$ pint milk

Rub the fat in the flour, then add the currants, sugar, peel and mixed spice. Add sufficient milk to make into a soft dough. Roll out to half an inch thickness and cut to shape with a round cutter. Brush with beaten egg to glaze and bake at about 350°F for 10 to 15 minutes. These are nice split and spread with butter.

CORNISH FRUIT LOAF

1 cupful dried fruit (sultanas and currants)	1 cupful tea
	1 beaten egg
1 cupful demerara sugar	2 cupfuls self-raising flour

Soak the fruit and sugar in a cupful of warm tea overnight. Next day add the flour and beaten egg. Bake in a lined oblong cake tin for about 30 minutes at 375°F. Best eaten the next day, sliced and buttered. It is also very good toasted and buttered.

FAIRINGS

4 ozs butter	2 tsps baking powder
4 ozs sugar	2 tsps bicarbonate of soda
8 ozs flour	2 tsps mixed spice
4 tbsps golden syrup	3 tsps ground ginger
$\frac{1}{2}$ tsp salt	1 tsp cinnamon

Sieve together the flour, salt, spices, baking powder and bicarbonate of soda. Rub in the butter and add the sugar. Spoon the syrup into a cup, stand in shallow water in a pan and heat gently until soft. Pour the liquid syrup on to the other ingredients and work in thoroughly. Flour the hands and roll the mixture into small balls. Place on a greased baking tray, well spaced out. Bake at 400°F, moving the biscuits from the top to the bottom shelf of the oven the moment they begin to brown.

YEAST RECIPES, QUICK BREADS & SCONES

BROWN OATMEAL BREAD

1 lb flour	4 tbsps coarse oatmeal
2 ozs lard	1 tsp salt
Sour milk	1 tsp bicarbonate of soda

Sieve together the salt, bicarbonate of soda and flour and mix very thoroughly. Rub in the fat until like fine breadcrumbs, then mix in the oatmeal. Make a well in the middle of the mixture, add some very sour milk until a dry, spongy dough is produced—a sticky one will make the bread heavy. Turn on to a floured board, divide into two pieces and quickly pat or roll the dough into two flat cakes. Place on a couple of floured baking trays. Score each cake lightly into four quarters with a knife and bake for 30 minutes at 425°F.

OATMEAL SCONES

6 ozs flour	Good pinch salt
2 ozs medium oatmeal	2 ozs butter
$\frac{1}{2}$ tsp bicarbonate of soda	Sour milk
$\frac{1}{2}$ tsp cream of tartar	

Carefully sieve together the flour, salt, bicarbonate of soda and the cream of tartar. Rub in the fat with the fingertips. Make a well in the centre of the mixture and gradually add the milk to form a soft and spongy dough which 'cleans' the basin and yet is not sticky. Quickly and lightly roll out on a floured board to about one inch thickness. Cut into rounds, place on a floured baking tray and bake for about 8 minutes at 450°F.

CORNISH SPLITS

2 ozs lard
1 lb white flour
1 tsp salt

1 oz yeast
1 tsp castor sugar
½ pint milk

Warm the milk. Cream the sugar and yeast together and mix with the milk. Sieve together the flour and salt, rub in the lard and add all this to the liquid mixture to form a soft dough. Knead thoroughly, leave in a warm place to rise, knead again and then shape into round buns. Lightly flour a baking tray, leave to prove once more, then bake for about 15 minutes at 400°F.

Splits can be served hot, cut open and buttered, or cold with clotted cream and jam.

SODA BREAD

8 ozs wholemeal flour
8 ozs white flour
1 oz butter
½ pint buttermilk

1 tsp salt
1 tsp cream of tartar
1 tsp bicarbonate of
  soda

Sieve together the flour, salt, cream of tartar and bicarbonate of soda. Rub in the fat. Make a well in the middle and add buttermilk until a soft, dry dough is produced. Divide into two, and form each piece into a round flat cake on a floured board. Score each lightly with a knife into quarters and bake on a floured tray at 400°F for about half an hour, until risen and brown.

CHEESY BREAD

8 ozs flour
1 tsp salt
3 tsps baking powder
Milk

4 ozs grated Cheddar
  cheese
4 ozs mashed and sieved
  potatoes

Sieve together the flour, baking powder and salt, making sure there are no lumps remaining, particularly of the baking powder. Gradually add the finely grated cheese and the sieved potatoes, blending the mixture quickly with the finger tips. Add enough milk to make a soft, dry dough and make into small rounds, handling as little as possible. Place on a floured tray and bake for about 15 minutes at 450°F.

CURRANT SCONES

8 ozs flour	Good pinch salt
2 ozs butter	$\frac{1}{4}$ pint milk
2 ozs currants	1 tsp cream of tartar
$\frac{1}{2}$ tsp bicarbonate of soda	

Sieve together the flour, cream of tartar, bicarbonate of soda and the salt. Rub in the fat lightly, and add the currants. Form a well in the mixture and add sufficient milk to form a spongy, dry dough. Knead gently for a moment, place on a floured board and lightly roll out to about three quarters of an inch thick. Cut into rounds, arrange on a floured tray and bake at 450°F for about 10 minutes.

CURRANTY BREAD

$2\frac{1}{2}$ lbs white flour	1 lb currants
1 oz yeast	1 pint milk
2 ozs candied peel	$\frac{1}{2}$ oz castor sugar
2 ozs lard	2 tsps salt

Sieve together the flour and salt. Rub in the fat until like fine breadcrumbs and then add the chopped-up peel and the fruit. Then take the yeast, cream it with the sugar and mix in with the milk. Pour the liquid into a well made in the centre of the flour, cover it with a sprinkling of the flour, place a clean tea-towel over the bowl and leave in a warm place for 30 minutes. Then carefully mix to a soft dough, knead thoroughly and leave again in a warm place until twice the size. Cut into about four pieces to half fill several greased and floured tins. Place once more in a warm spot until the dough has risen to fill the tins. Bake for a quarter of an hour at 450°F, then a further hour at 375°F.

YEAST CURRANT LOAF

1 lb flour	1 egg
2 ozs butter	4 ozs currants
2 ozs lard	2 ozs sultanas or
1 level tsp salt	candied peel
$\frac{3}{4}$ oz yeast	A little nutmeg
About $\frac{1}{2}$ pint milk	4 ozs sugar

Sieve the flour and the salt together and rub in the fat. Add the sugar. Cream the yeast with a spoon until liquefied. Warm the milk and pour on to the beaten egg. Add this to the yeast and pour the mixture on to the flour. Beat well and set aside in a warm place, covered, to rise. After about one hour mix in the fruit, candied peel and nutmeg. Divide into two greased loaf tins and set into a warm place to 'prove', or rise, and fill the tins. Bake for about 15 minutes at 400°F and then at about 25 minutes at 350°F.

CHEESE SCONES

4 ozs flour	1 tsp baking powder
$\frac{1}{2}$ oz butter	Pinch salt and pepper
1 oz cheese	$\frac{1}{8}$ pint milk

Sieve together the flour, baking powder, salt and pepper. Rub in the butter. Grate and add the cheese. Add the milk to make a soft dough. Knead and shape to about half an inch thick. Mark into quarters with a knife, brush with milk and bake for about 10 minutes at 425°F.

SAFFRON CAKE

$\frac{1}{2}$ dram saffron	4 ozs sugar
2 lbs flour	1 lb currants
1 lb butter	1 oz yeast
2 ozs candied peel	Warm milk
Pinch of salt	

Cut up the saffron and soak overnight by adding a little boiling water, which it will flavour and stain a bright orange. Rub the butter in the flour, add the salt, sugar, finely chopped peel and currants. Warm a little milk and pour it over the yeast and one teaspoonful of sugar in a basin. When the yeast rises, pour it into a well in the centre of the flour. Cover it with a sprinkling of the flour, and when the yeast rises through this and breaks it, mix the whole by hand into a dough, adding milk as needed, as well as the saffron water. Leave in a warm place to rise for a little while. Bake in a cake tin for about one hour at 350°F.

Saffron is obtained from the autumn-flowering *Crocus sativus* and is expensive to buy. This is because the plant is difficult to grow, being prone to disease and easily spoiled by high winds. Moreover, the stigmata of over 4,000 blooms are required to produce 1 oz (16 drams) of saffron.

BEVERAGES

CORNISH MEAD

3 lbs honey   1 oz yeast
2 ozs root ginger   1 gallon water

Boil the water for half an hour before use, then add the honey and boil for one hour more, skimming off any scum that may rise. Cut up the ginger and bruise it (Jamaica ginger is best). Place it in a muslin bag and add to the liquid. When almost cold add the yeast. Bottle, and when it has finished working, cork tightly.

Mead can be drunk hot or cold. The longer it is kept the better.

SLOE WINE

4 pints sloes   4 lbs granulated sugar
4 pints water

Ensure only ripe, black sloes are used, but make certain none are shrivelled. Pour boiling water over the sloes in a large container and leave to soak for a week in a warm place. Stir the mixture twice a day. Add the sugar gradually and stir thoroughly until dissolved. Bottle and cork loosely, then tighten the corks when the working is finished. Keep at least six months before use.

CORNISH BARM

$\frac{1}{2}$ cup flour   2 pints water
$\frac{1}{2}$ cup mashed potato $\frac{1}{2}$ cup sugar

Mix together the mashed potato, flour and sugar. Add the water (warmed), also a few raisins. Bottle, and leave for at least one week before using.

MAHOGANY

Mix together one cup of treacle with two of gin. Beat well. Traditionally this drink was served with 'fair maids' or pilchards.

HARVEST DRINK (SPRUCE)

1 lb sugar	2 tsps tartaric acid
1 gallon water	1 tsp ground ginger
Half a lemon	

Dissolve the sugar in one pint of the water (boiling). Add the other ingredients, including the juice of the lemon and the chopped up rind. Dilute to one gallon with the rest of the water (cold).

ELDERFLOWER WINE

2 pints elderflowers	2 ozs wine yeast
2 gallons water	8 lbs brown sugar
4 lemons	About $\frac{1}{4}$ lb root
4 oranges	ginger

Thinly slice the fruit into a large earthenware or plastic container, add the ginger, lightly bruised, the elder flowers and the sugar. Boil the water and pour on to these ingredients. Allow to cool slightly and add the yeast. Leave to stand for several days, stirring twice a day. Then strain carefully through clean muslin. Bottle and cork. After about six weeks, store the bottles in a cool dark cupboard on their sides.